Distant Echoes

'All our dreams, fragile things, floating on the bosom of emptiness.'

by

Martin Richards

authorHOUSE™

1663 Liberty Drive, Suite 200
Bloomington, Indiana 47403
(800) 839-8640
www.AuthorHouse.com

© 2005 Martin Richards. All Rights Reserved.

No part of this book may be reproduced, stored in a retrieval system, or transmitted by any means without the written permission of the author.

First published by AuthorHouse 07/27/05

ISBN: 1-4208-5907-2 (sc)

Printed in the United States of America
Bloomington, Indiana

This book is printed on acid-free paper.

Acknowledgements

Thanks to darling wife Ann-Marie for her continued
Support and inspiration

Special Thanks to
Mike, Susie and Carol
When print began

Contents

Foreword xiii

Romantic Poems

Woman! 2
Love's Anxiety 4
Temptation 5
My Lover's Questions 6
No One Else Would Do 7
Love's Dilemma 8
For What Is Love? 10
Searching for Reasons 12
Missing You 13
A Commitment to Love 15
Love Wishes 16
Lost Without You 17

Nostalgic Poems

Nostalgia 20
Drum Beat 21
It Seems Like Yesterday 22
Beautiful Brothers of Mine 24
Carnival 26
Gone 27
Failure 28

Philosophical Poems

Scattered Pieces 30
For What is Life? 31
Echoes From the Wilderness 32
Cries in the Wilderness 33
The Dancers 34
Sonnet For A Lady 36
Quest 37
Little Flower 38
Give Me A Reason 39
By Reason of Insanity 40
This Course of Life 41
Food for Thought 42
Revolution 43
Wanted 44
Liberation 46
Fleeting Impressions 47
Bad Vibrations 48
Soul Searching 49
Hold on To Your Dreams 50
Choose or Lose 52
Slow Down 53
Where Are The People 54
Blank Pages 56
Why Is Peace So Illusive? 57

Homeless 58
Enigma 60
Reality 61
The Reality of Dreams 62
This Modern Life, Another Look 64
Modern Life 66
The Playground 67
Paradoxes 68
You and Me 69

Social Commentary

Letter From the Homeless 72
Thinking About the Children 74
Have You Seen My Son? 76
Innocent Ones 78
Nightmare! 79
The Wall 80
The Writing Is On The Wall 81
Just One Wish 83
I Hear A Cry! 84
Life on the Edge 85
Shattered Dreams 86
Mislead 88
After the Smoke Clears 89
Enigma of A Lady 90
People 92

Dear Brother and Sister 93
Somebody Cares 95
City of the Dead 97

Existential Poems
To Be Me 100
I Am Not Me 102
Searching 104
Leave Me In The Dark 106
Beggar-man 108
Poetic Dilemma 109
Let the Music Play 111
The Traveler 112
Heart Songs 114
I'd Rather Be Blind 116
The Watcher 118
My Soul Looks Back And Wonder 119

Miscellaneous Poems
There is a Mouse in My Room 122
Shoes 123
Rain 124
Haiku 125
My Son's Birth 126
Clouds 127
Poetry 128

Snow	129
The Rain	130
The Musical Rain	131
Waiting for Spring	132
Winter and Me	133
Pages	134
The Wind and Me	135
Nostalgia	136
Dreams	137
Journey	138
When I was Little	140
Spring	141
Dem Dun Forget	142
What Do You Want To Be?	143
Summer's Heat	144
One Wish	145
The Education Plan	146
Wishing for you	147

Foreword

This anthology depicts a journey of words across the threshold of my life. I can well remember that day, when I sat in a restaurant in Port of Spain, Trinidad looking at the passersby. I was drawn to their faces and their expressions, and I began to write my first poem attempting to capture their moods and feelings in words. Since then I've stared both birth and death in the face as I have traveled across the mountains and valleys of life.

My poems are the scriptive representation of my inner thoughts and my interpretation of life, its beauty and lack of. As I ponder and contemplate the vastness of the universe in the light of scientific evidence of a world that has been in existence for billions of years, I am filled with awe. I am awed at the tremendous expanse of it all and how infinitesimal we are.

WHO ARE WE? WHERE ARE WE GOING? We struggle and strive for 'things', which in the larger scope of life are nothing but dust, relics of our greed and selfishness, and our inability to let love be the focal point of all of our actions. How long will the blind continue to lead the blind? How long will we allow ourselves to be led by those who swim in the seas of corruption and prejudice? When will we free ourselves from the thinking of the collective consciousness? When will we awaken from the sleep of ignorance?

Like the ancient prophets and soothsayers, I too proclaim a message in my writings. My voice also joins theirs, as I hear the 'Distant Echoes' of the voices of those who have crossed over, their cries are for all of us to turn fro have and strife and live in harmony. But can we? Can the creature change is habits? When will we stop the masquerade and allow ourselves to truly live.

Martin Richards

Romantic Poems

*'When two become one
Love is the only true bond'*

Woman!

Woman!
Of my dreams,
My emotional screams,
Mystic woman it seems,

You haunt,
You taunt,
You flaunt,

Woman!
You sway,
In my way,
Mind games you play

You make me glad,
Yet sad,
And mad.

Woman!
Ah! So neat,
Passion's treat,
My life complete.

You ignite the fire,
Fueled by love's desire,
Potent as an electric wire,

Woman!
Ah! Too much tension,
Twisting the chords of emotion,
My mind lost in sweet oblivion,

Your body turns,
My inside churns,
The flame burns,

Woman!

Love's Anxiety

I cannot wait,
Thoughts of you only aggravate,
The yearning that burns,
Like a plunging river it churns,
As anxiety controls,
Adrenalin flows,
Waiting! The pain grows.

No sedation,
For the eager anticipation,
As time, like a colossal burden,
Strains the chords of reason,
Pressing me closer to insanity,
A frightening probability.

In my mouth, no saliva,
Yet I can taste the desire,
Of love's tenderness,
As my mind abodes,
In the realm of emotional bliss.

Like a child yearning for a Christmas toy,
I am consumed with the joy,
Of homo-sapiens pleasure,
And the warmth of our bodies together.

Temptation

It's futile to resist,
The gift,
Wrapped in subtle provocation,
Hidden passionate emotion
Dormant,
Mirrored obscurity,
Ah! To caress and rest,
Then quietly savor,
The thrill
Of biological conquest,
Desire burns,
Curtailed
By eyed expectancy,
Only to ignite,
When paths cross,
And vibrations transgress,
With nearness,
And electric proximity,
Heart beat - fast,
Creature anxiety,
Floating,
Floating on air.

My Lover's Questions

You wonder if I still love you,
Whether or not my feelings are still true blue?
Or whether or not there is an 'other'?
You say you want to hear those immortal words
from my lips,
Not from my poetry, pen and paper,
But these objects are but pawns, instruments,
Tools, caught up in the game of love,
Which my heart uses to express,
The totality of its fullness,
With a love I've not known before,
A love that's so much more,
Beyond the definitions of language,
Living in realms of bliss and happiness,
Freedom and satiety.

No One Else Would Do

I'd rather be
With you, than any other place,
Savoring the smile,
That radiates from your beautiful face.

I'd rather be
With you, than experience another day,
When time shows no mercy or compassion,
My mind in emotional oblivion.

I'd rather be
With you, no one else seems adequate,
Or able to sedate,
The fire of love that burns.

I'd rather be
With you hypnotized by your spell,
Feeling the warmth of your touch,
And the other things you do so well.

I'd rather be
With you, no other's arms are able,
Or capable, to quench the yearning,
To be loved.

Love's Dilemma

Sweetheart,
Distance is measured in miles,
Weight from ounces to tons,
There is volume, area,
And linear measure.

But what's the yardstick for my love so true?
Is my love for you far?
Is it light or heavy?
Is it high, wide or lengthy - or voluminous?

How could I get an accurate readout?
Of my love which you cannot doubt?
What are the coordinates?
What is the longitude, the latitude?
Or even my love's altitude?

How do I gauge or quantify?
Is it yards of love?
What is its' radius?
How long, how wide?
Is this feeling that churns on my inside?

Sweetheart,
Temperature is measured in Celsius or Fahrenheit,
But to say my love is hot or cold,

At freezing point or boiling point,
Would that be right?

Is there a known way to appraise, valuate or assess?
Feelings that have filled a void, an emptiness,
Is it a pint or quart,
A gallon or a liter?
Is my love for you an acre?

How could I best measure,
My love's size or stature?
Is huge or small,
Short or tall?

What could I use to calibrate,
Or accurately calculate,
To span and fathom,
My love to the absolute angstrom?

Just how do you measure love?
How does one truly compute,
Beyond refute,
Add or subtract,
The totality of a feeling.

For What Is Love?

Is it the ultimate emotional adventure?
We share with the other partner,
Wherein lies secrets rare and uncommonly,
Satisfaction being the only key,

Is it the physical fantasy?
That transports you away from reality,
Such sweet, sweet mental abduction,
As you ride high on the wings of this addiction,

Is it the true blue feeling?
That sends your heart reeling,
Escalating your emotions to the sky,
Feelings, sensations, uncontrollable - Why?

Is it the beauty of that feeling?
Radiant as a new day dawning,
Beautiful, real and true,
But more often disappears as the morning dew.

Is love more or higher?
That flamboyant desire,
Is it more than physical adoration?
And fulfilling of each sporadic emotion,

Is it more than youthful infatuation?
That soft spot, or casual flirtation,
Is it in the cherished memories?
And the nostalgic idiosyncrasities.

Searching for Reasons

Why do I love like I do?
Your smile,
Your kisses too,

Why do I long for the way you hug and caress?
Your touch,
Your sweet tenderness,

Why for your companionship I yearn?
Your support,
Your care and concern,

Why has loving you made such a difference?
Your style,
Your emotional sustenance,

Why do you haunt my every thought?
Your intuitiveness,
Your motivation, without which I am distraught,

I guess I can't help searching for reasons,
Trying to add and subtract the totality,
Of my love for you darling.

Missing You

Right now I lay and think of you,
Building pictures in my mind,
Which are not hard to find,
As I strive to imagine where you are,
Clouds, miles of water,
The distance ....
Oh! So far.

With each passing day I think more of you,
Memories,
They all seem so brand new,
Was our happiness a dream?
Was it true?
Or a puff of smoke,
Evaporating as the strong wind blew?

Across snow covered landscapes,
Though bare,
Yet images of your face are everywhere,
Your voice even calls out to me,
Ah! Love's haunting malady,
Everything I do,
Somehow seems to recall memories of you.

Time and time again,
As I walk in the cold, cold rain,

I can feel the pain,
As the hurt grows,
Of joys as distant as the miles;
Emotional desperation,
Driving my mind into oblivion.

What a fool was I to play,
Thinking I could runaway,
Take a holiday,
From love;
Your see baby,
Love for you is still the way it used to be,
Glowing deep within the heart of me.

A Commitment to Love

In spite of what I think is wrong with you,
Which in reality,
Is what is wrong with me;
Faults and doubts which surge within,
These I rarely see or acknowledge,
I will love you.

What is wrong with the world?
But in reality it is what is wrong with me,
For the people, the places,
The world, and the numerous faces,
Are reflections of me,
I will love you.

Despite your imperfections,
You are a mirror image of me,
For every time I look at you,
The frowns, the frustrations, the anxiety,
Unknowingly, it is my reflection I see,
I will love you.

Once I begin to see you differently,
And I continue to love you,
I also love me,
In quiet acceptance of you,
I also accept me,
This is the key, a state of non-duality,
I will love you.

Love Wishes

This has to be right,
Because every time I see you,
My sanity takes flight,
Feelings, emotions so real
Words can't truly express the way I feel

The sun seems to shine so much brighter,
Your face, your smile,
Radiant as a spring flower,
Oh! How I wish I could savor,
Their radiance forever,

No one knows, how much,
I am under your spell,
Should I really tell?
I wish time would stand still,
Leaving me forever under your will;

What am I to do?
Seems like eternity,
When I don't see you,
Just a touch, a smile,
And the waiting seems worthwhile.

Lost Without You

Yesterday, I knocked on your door,
But, no one,
No one answered!
My heart fell to the floor.

I didn't know what to do,
Afraid to face the world alone,
I felt so helpless,
Lost, without you;

I tried to imagine,
Where you could be,
But this only added to the insanity,
Love's painful apoplexy;

You see darling,
When the world turns me away,
Your love, your arms offer the serenity,
That gives me the strength to fight another day.

Nostalgic Poems

'Time, the bandit has stolen my years, sweeping them under the rug of my memory'.

Nostalgia

Oh! How I long to journey,
To the place of my nativity,
Where the yellow orb shines inhibited,
And fun is free,
Not a high-priced commodity.

Oh! I could hear the rain's characteristic melody,
Where nature blooms with fervency,
The bugs eager to satisfy their curiosity,
Ah! Such a vivid fantasy,
Masquerading in reality.

Oh! Land where the full moon makes the darkness flee,
The fire flies soar like heaven's missiles,
And the night bird's haunting call,
Sends children to sleep,
To dream of ghosts and spirits.

Oh! Land that beckons,
Mother, to my native instincts,
Of tears, of fears,
Where the ties of ancestry mingles with the dust,
Beneath a holy marker.

Oh! It is I your prodigal son,
Estranged where opportunity once reigned,
And the LADY beckoned,
Now tainted by bigotry and disharmony,
Tropical breezes the only remedy.

Land! Of an enviable sunset,
The opium for my loneliness,
The potent portion,
To cure the longings –
To see familiar faces,
Of a common lineage.

Drum Beat

Drums, drums
Distant drums I hear,
Original, natural drums
Rhythm,
Fire,
Shango,
Drums, from the Congo.

Drums, drums,
Drums beat,
Fast,
Stir my soul,
Can't stop my feet,
Momentum,
Rhythm,
Ritual, survival,

Drums, drums,
Drums beat,
Music,
Ancestral messages,
To my soul, calling across the sea,
Compelling, commanding,
Livid, vivid,

Drums beat.

It Seems Like Yesterday

It seems like yesterday,
I was just a boy,
My immediate fancy a brand new toy;

It seems like yesterday,
When I could savor,
The sweet juices of the cashew and the guava;

I remember those red and blue striped pajamas I wore,
When I was ten years old.

It seems like yesterday,
When I could fish with an old tin can,
In the ravine, for Cascarob and Guabin;

It seems like yesterday,
When the sun baked street,
Showed no mercy to my shoeless feet;

I can still remember the dust on my hands,
As I pitched marbles under the mango tree;
It seems like yesterday,
When I scrubbed and mopped the floors,
Ah! Such tedious chores;

I can still hear the anxiety in my mother's call,
As my brothers and I played football.

It seems like yesterday,
When the squawks of corn-birds squabbling,
Signaled a new day dawning;

It seems like yesterday,
I fell from the breadfruit tree,
Bitten by Jack Spaniard, as I tried to flee;

I can still hear the night bird's haunting shriek,
Goose pimples! From under the sheet I would peek,
It seems as though only one day has gone by,
Why did time fly?

Beautiful Brothers of Mine

Fresh are the memories of yesterday,
How I remember,
The times we walked and talked,
No real cares or concerns,
When we looked at life through a mirror,
Only seeing the happiness of youth;
Youth! So free and happy,
Unconcerned about maturity.

Beautiful brothers of mine,
I can still recall,
When we played football,
Those cuts and bruises,
Times we bathed in the rain,
Worked ……… carried water,
Cleaned the yard,
Chores, that then seemed, oh! So hard.

That old house,
A sibling monument,
Our refuge,
Gone ………..
Like our youth,
Eaten by time's voracious appetite;
Those times we went to school,
Yeah! Just played the fool.

Somehow there's pain in my heart,
Why did youth depart?
Why can't we have those joys of boyhood?
To smile, laugh and run,
And just have fun?
Yet everyday I pray,
That God will keep and guide you,
In all you do;

I guess I'll never understand,
Only time will tell and give answers,
To those faded glories,
My treasured memories,
That seem,
Like puffs of smoke,
Blown away by maturity;

Beautiful brothers of mine,
I long to see you,
To talk, and reminisce,
About youth's bliss.
Though time has separated us,
And life with new commitments,
Our hearts are yet like one,
Love our true bond.

Carnival

Music, music,
Music everywhere,
Time to jump, jump,
No reason to fear;

Steel bands, steel bands,
Steel bands everywhere,
Sweet steel bands,
Making havoc with my ear;

Masqueraders, masqueraders,
Masqueraders, ah! So pretty,
Colors! Gone crazy!
Such livid, vivid beauty;

People, people,
People under a watchful sun,
Absorbed in the fun,
Sick! With Carnival fever;

Dance, dance,
Dance to the calypso,
Natural rhythm, come, step to the tempo;
Bacchanal! Noise, noise for so;

Carnival, carnival,
Carnival, ah! Creole ecstasy,
Cultural insanity,
But a delightful malady.

Gone

No more,
The sun shines,
Through every crack and crevice,
Only gloom and darkness reigns,
Among disheveled rooms
And decaying walls;

No more,
The rippling peals of laughter and gaiety,
The buzzing hum of human activity,
Fill the air,
Only silence,
Still and heavy,
Nothing but a strange unfriendly wind;

No more,
The feet of men and women
Tramp out footprints,
They too, are gone,
Overgrown by shrubs and bushes;
Even the vines find repose,
On walls whose spirits have been broken;

No more the tops of walls and huts,
Stand predominant,
Against the horizon,
Just a lush forest,
Green life,
Amidst the ruins;

No more,
The nearby river's fervent flow,
In interrupted,
But on and on unceasingly,
A twisted journey,
Fathering new life,
On its eternal journey.

Failure

When I was a lad,
Failure often made me mad,
Sometimes even sad,
But never, never glad.

 I would often cry and grieve,
As I couldn't bring myself to believe,
My mind couldn't conceive,
I was much too naïve;

Even though I was young,
And each failure made me frown,
My faith somehow remained strong,
Yet something would invariably go wrong;

Try as I might,
My sanity often took flight,
I would sometimes lose the will to fight,
It just didn't seem right;

That failure didn't mean I was a failure,
Or to others inferior,
Neither was I a born loser,
It just meant I had to try harder.

Philosophical Poems

*'All of our dreams, fragile things,
floating on the bosom of emptiness*

Scattered Pieces

Which way is up?
Our lives fragments, scattered pieces,
Out of touch,
Disconnected from ourselves;
We are anxious, restless,
Children of neuroses,
And the illusions of ego,
A minor crisis often pricks the balloon of our existence;

Deep seated hurts and fears,
Continually shadow and existence –
Of suspense and ambiguity;
We run, hiding behind familiar social facades,
Plunging ourselves into creature addictions,
Futile attempts at anonymity;
Happiness rides on the unsaddled back,
Of sporadic good fortune,
How do we discover meaning amidst the meaningless?

For What is Life?

For what is life?
How best should se assess this reality?
Dream or illusion,
Plagued with suffering and confusion?

Is there 'something' behind the appearances?
 The nuances,
Of perceptual differences,
That we are yet to discern?

Must we just live and die?
A hapless existence,
Survival the only motivation,
Despite blatant greed and confusion,

Who has perhaps and answer?
Or a lamp?
To shed light in the midst of the darkness,
The senselessness, of hatred and global strife,

Just birth and death,
A preposition so meaningless,
A sad aberration,
For those who continually grasp at the illusion,

For what is life?
Journey or destiny,
Is love and compassion,
Perhaps the answer to the delusion?

Echoes From the Wilderness

Oh! Cruel world,
Can't you see the poor?
They are everywhere,
In each and every hemisphere,
They are there,
Enigmas of a status quo
That continually oppress;

Oh! Cruel world,
Can't you hear their Cries??
Listen, you'll hear,
As they cry for succor,
Their bellies churning,
With an empty agony,
By the thousands they die daily;

Oh! Cruel world,
Can't you hear the poor?
Their cries arise from every culture,
Above historical persuasion,
Into desperate unanimity,
For greed like a runaway train is rampant,
To their cries we are often nonchalant;

Oh! Cruel world,
The knife of their despair,
Cuts deep into the fabric of our democracy,
What a difference it would be,
If wealth was shared equally,
And LOVE was what it should be,
Indeed we would have a better world.

Cries in the Wilderness

Can you hear ……..
The cries?
Cries in the wilderness,
Cries of injustice,
Corruption and oppression,
Ethnic blindness ……….

Stop! Listen,
You'll hear,
Silent screams of fear,
Invisible desperation,
Many grasping for a chance to fully live,
Is it so hard for us to give?

Everywhere,
Loud decibels,
A crescendo of voices,
Deserted,
Calling,
Hoping, longing,

Are you listening?

The Dancers

Decorated, disguised, preoccupied,
They dance,
As if,
The dance is their existence;

While opportunity slips away like the darkness at dawn,
They dance;
As if,
Dancing is living;

Though others seek the academic, the prolific,
They dance,
As if,
The dance, will their lives enhance;

To the pulsation, the rhythm,
They dance,
As if,
Dancing will hush the voices that are crying;

Hunger, chaos, order – disorder,
They dance,
As if,
The dance will induce a trance;

While many languish on the shores of self pity,
They dance,
As if,
Dancing is their motivation:

Tireless, unconcerned,
They dance,
As if,
The dance will alter life's unfairness, its imbalance;

Their bodies in musical harmony,
They dance,
As if,
This numbs the pains as they prance;

Global strife, abuse, misuse,
They dance,
As if,
Dancing nullifies the suffering.

Sonnet For A Lady

*I saw a woman crying today,
I tried to assure her that tomorrow may not be this way,
In a soft voice I heard her mutter,
Your words ring true but they are empty,
As through these troubled years,
I've become conversant with life's adversity,
Yet I can't restrain the tears,
I have heard such tedium before,
All my efforts at self - help are in vain,
As trouble invariably knocks at my door,
Even religion cannot fully explain,
In reply I had to admit,
Life is arduous and uncertain,
But should you relinquish and quit?*

Quest

Man,
Ever searching,
Seeking,
The true earth,
Void of sadness and mirth;

But where is it?
Reality or illusion,
Despite modern innovation,
The brotherhood of man cannot materialize,
Though many preach and emphasize,
Peace and love,
As exemplified by the 'One above',

Yet,
No one listens,
Or see the hand that beckons,
Amidst the ordered madness,
They are trapped, swayed by a collective consciousness;

But,
Many still dream and set forth,
The quest is still for utopia,
Seemingly near,
Like the proverbial butterfly,
But oh! So far.

Little Flower

Little flower,
There you are,
Untroubled, untouched by the madness,
Short lived happiness,
Oblivious,
To the obvious;

I wish I could wear your smile,
In a world so vile,
Be radiant in the sun,
Though nothing is being done
To halt the addiction,
To scientific invention,
Fruitless to the problems that plague man;

Little flower,
There you are,
Untainted by the malice,
While injustice,
Prejudice, and inequality,
Reign triumphantly,
Dissipating the structure,
The morals and values that once bonded us together;

How could I appreciate your beauty?
When my heart is heavy,
Shackled by global poverty,
My mind in turmoil and disarray,
All around, nothing but decay,
Please share with me your secret,
Before I lose my wit.

Give Me A Reason

Is there a reason to live?
When the beauty of a flower is insignificant,
When the rain becomes a bother,
And no matter the weather,
You feel blue;

Is there a reason to live?
When clouds seem to always obscure the sun,
When just as life is getting better,
Invariably fate would have its way,
And spoil the fun;

Is there a reason to live?
When no matter the way you choose,
Every which way you seem to lose,
When a smile clothes the tears,
Of your daily foreboding and fears;

Is there a reason to live?
When food seems to lose its flavor,
And nothing can savor,
Or fill the void –
The insatiable hunger;

Is there a reason to live?
When sleep flees from the darkness,
And you wonder,
When the past haunts,
And you are thoughts helpless prisoner;

Is there a reason to live?
When despair and frustration,
Becomes your shadowy companion,
When the agony, the anguish to survive,
Keep you searching for a reason to stay alive.

By Reason of Insanity

In a restless world as this,
Who truly cares?
Are we not all self-centered?
Parented by the illusions of our ego,
Programmed by desires and addictions,
Irregardless as to the consequences,
We harbor ill feelings towards our fellowman,
Cold, cold,
Children of callous parents;

Conditional pseudo love,
To each his own, her own,
Random values,
Situational ethics,
Many voices,
Eschewing from the chaos,
But who listens,
Yet we search,
Unsure, uncertain,
Is this reality?
Or the other side of sanity;

No more true laughter,
Forgotten, empty smiles,
The weeping faces of poverty,
And homelessness,
Haunt and stare,
Whispers,
Quiet desperation,
But who are we?
Innocent or guilty,
We act, we live,
By reason of insanity.

This Course of Life

This course of life,
Is never devoid of strife,
But is often inundated,
Sometimes seemingly obliterated,
By mountainous peaks of unfulfilled dreams,
And aspirations;
Valleys,
Carved out of frustrations;

Depressions,
Watered by the winding rivers of tribulations,
On whose banks,
Grow fertile forests of indecision,
In which huge trees of fear and doubt bloom,
And are allowed to mushroom;

Out of the forests,
One must traverse the futile deserts
Of loneliness,
With their mirages of happiness,
Oases of painted smiles and laughter;

Be weary of the cracks and crevices of failure,
The thorny bushes of mistakes,
That cut and torture,
Strive to avoid the sharp stones of society,
That cut at the strands of your sanity,
The upgrades and downgrades,
Of messed up responsibility,
Wait not for or expect sympathy,
For you are a participant in this puzzling reality.

Food for Thought

Whatever promotes the dignity of all men,
Ensures justice and equality,
Breaks the barriers, the barbed wires that defines
Race or class, and provides equanimity,
Think on these things;

Whatever, will cause wars to cease, curtail crime,
And criminal intent,
Dismantle, the machines of hate and distrust,
Is right, pure, good and promotes love and tolerance,
Think on these things;

Whatever, enhances the brotherhood of all men,
Eradicates waste, destroys greed and selfishness,
Will cause those blinded by centuries of corruption,
'To see', the shadows of the past,
Think on these things;

Whatever unmasks, lays naked the truth,
Uplifts the downtrodden, salvages freedom,
Outlaws mental, emotional, and physical abuse,
Think on these things;

Whatever, wipes away the tears, soothes the pain,
Of hunger and disharmony,
Restores laughter, the smiles of the children,
Recreates the rhythm of all life,
Think on these things.

Whatever motivates, uncovers the good in each of us,
Causes love to become the focal point that defines every action,
And makes us one with all of creation,
Think on these things.

Revolution

Where there is human domination,
Racial or social oppression,
Starvation or political suppression,
There will be revolution.

Within or without,
Nurturing, ready to sprout;

Wherever the dignity of man is allowed to decay,
To rot and fester away,
And be swallowed up in oblivion,
There will be revolution.

Shut up inside,
Until, there is no place to hide;

Wherever human feelings cannot be expressed,
But rather, it is oppressed
By laws and popular opinion,
There will be revolution.

The winds of time may come and blow,
But hopes and desires will someday glow;

Wherever man cannot be at his best,
Dreams and aspirations will not rest,
And though freedom may seem like an illusion,
There will be revolution.

Burning, burning bright,
Waiting, for men its spark to ignite.

Wanted

Men and women,
Of strong moral fiber,
Distinguished by the quality of their character;

Not by their position on the corporate ladder,
Or notoriety in the media;

Men and women,
Who are of no particular persuasion,
But whose lives are examples of their conviction;

Not those who pray and preach,
Failing to practice what they continually teach;

Men and women,
Who hold fast to the tenements of truth and honesty,
Conspicuous for their integrity;

Not those who delve in impropriety,
And are yet worshipped by society;

Men and women,
Radicals by popular opinion,
But whose beliefs in the universal brotherhood of man,
Is their unshaken confession;

Not today's heroes - pathetic, a sideshow relic,
Fickle, suicidal, synthetic;

Men and women,
Who with one chance encounter,
Can crush the barrier, that distinguishes race and culture,

*Not those who blow, like reeds in the wind,
Every which way, they continually sway;*

*Men and women,
Common everyday people,
Who can identify with the struggle;*

*Not the pessimistic or negative,
But those who can motivate you to live and
forgive.*

Liberation

Liberation, freedom
A common cry today,
As man seeks to escape,
And break, the chains,
Of oppression and racial segregation,
To eradicate universal strife,
Hatred and hunger,
And enhance life;

Men seek freedom, liberation,
To save a dying world,
From a polluted environment,
To abolish nuclear energy,
As they catch glimpses of what is imminent ....
Nuclear annihilation;

Liberation, freedom,
Protests, cries for charity,
Break these chains of inhumanity;
Is there a solution?
To the problem of ....
Alienation?

Fleeting Impressions

While mortals weep,
And bask themselves in kindred sleep,
Time will not wait,
Nor dreams, life's turmoil abate;
But fly ancient daughter,
Undaunted by moral matter,
Thrust for the unknown,
Despite each salient groan,
Ignore the lowly,
Heed that higher decree;
Let destiny dictate,
The commands of fate,
The pendulum must not delay,
Though mortals stare in dismay,
Time ..... the empty, the unknown,
Myriads of nothing ....

Bad Vibrations

Fallen leaves,
Skeleton trees,
Dressed up in white,
A distant train goes by,
The tracks seem to dance,
To a creaky whining melody;

Train, train,
Wait!
Don't hesitate,
To transport me,
From life's disharmony;
No music, no melody,
But salient tones,
Deep groans
Of suffering,
A crescendo of voices calling ....

Nothing but distortion,
Crazy vibrations,
Life, like an unchained melody;
No sharps or majors,
Only E minors,
And flats of despair;

Train, train,
Wait!
Don't hesitate,
To transport me,
Away! From this apoplexy;
To a future reality,
Modulating a new kind of melody,
A distinctive harmony.

Soul Searching

There is a hunger in man,
A seeming senseless,
Never-ending desire;
A relentless, restless searching,
Always looking for something;

In this bustling,
This fidgety,
This greedy world,
There is universal hunger,
An insatiable desire,
For something more;

No peace, or satisfaction,
To an unappeasing hunger;
The urge to possess,
To grab, to seize,
A philosophy of what's yours is mine,
To fill the void;
But yet,
No fulfillment,
Life that leads on interminably,
To death,
Of soul and body.

Hold on To Your Dreams

Dream,
Poor man,
Average man,
Hungry man,
Dream,
Enhance your self-esteem;

Dream!
It's your last hope,
To ride the ladder –
Of success;
Dream,
Less inequality,
The riches of the wealthy,
Hurl you into insanity;

Dream,
Don't cry,
Or stumble on Why?
Lost opportunity,
Look up and live;
Just dream,
Soothe the pains
Of your hungering – wanting,
Dream,
Lest failures,
Haunt and taunt;

Dream!
Ride high,
On the wings of fantasy,
Of palatial places,
Of the minority,
Who bask in plenty;

Dream,
Less tears,
Like poisonous things,
Stain and mar,
Ambition's desire;
And the knives of despair,
Discontentment - Cut,
Deep piercing wounds of resentment;

Dream dreams,
Don't let them die,
They are the seeds -
That flourish,
Amidst the madness,
Visual selfishness,
Blatant wantonness .....
Dream!

Choose or Lose

Choose or lose,
A chance to be,
To transform dream to reality,
Hopes and creature aspiration,
To fruition.

Choose or lose,
Disregard human error,
Each haunting failure,
Don't wallow in the squalor,
But ride high,
Climb the ladder,
Whose rungs ring out success;

Choose or lose,
Choices are natural,
At times Ah! So trivial,
But are they?
Who can say,
What they will uncover,
In an uncertain future;

Choose or lose,
Don't sit on the fence,
While the world spews in moral decadence,
Thrust aside the debris,
Grasp the opportunity "to be",

Choose or lose,
Don't stumble on why,
Reach for the sky,
Rise above the mundane,
And strive to gain
The coveted,
The unexpected;
Choose or lose,
It's up to you.

Slow Down

Amidst the hustle,
Your daily hassle,
With the demands of life,
The stress and strife,
There is still beauty –
Lurking, waiting,
Stop awhile and you'll see.

Take time,
Behold a flower,
Tune in to nature,
Say hello,
Even to a stranger,
Check the beauty of the sky,
Under which the birds fly.

Hey! Slow down,
Don't frown,
Check your stride,
You should be smiling,
Life is still worth living.

Hey! Brother, sister,
Slow down,
Let love be the motivating factor,
Even you can share and care,
Don't be paralyzed by fear,
The universe awaits.

Where Are The People

Where are the people?
People I used to know,
Seems a long time ago,
When they were governed by the moral,
The ethical,
Gone –
Swallowed up by the new ideology;

Where are the people?
Not the ones I now see,
Off springs of a fabricated society,
Modular patterns,
Geometric figurations,
Shells –
Void of compassion;

Where are the people?
Startling numbers,
Nostalgic replicas,
Catalogued in computers,
Like beings held captive,
Shadows –
Terrestrial enigmas;

Where are the people?
Men and women of character,
Who in the midst of difficulty,
Were distinguished by their reputability,
Their devotion to charity,
Habeas corpus –
Memories, in the archives of history;

Where are the people?
Who is guilty?
For man's present apoplexy,

Indicative to every culture,
Creator or creature;
Bewilderment –
No answers to these troubling questions;

Where are the people?
What caused their demise?
Who can eulogize?
A once proud creation,
Now, imminent destruction,
Alienation –
A new earth, a new creation.

Blank Pages

Pages,
Blank pages,
Void of scriptive activity,
Just lines –
On a horizontal journey,
Waiting!

For someone to write,
With words incite,
And invite,
Some reader,
With thoughts and ideas,
Which perchance might,
Shed light,
On ignorance,
And enhance,
Intellectualism.

Why Is Peace So Illusive?

I wish someone could tell me,
Why in the twenty first century,
Our eyes can't discern the true reality;
Nation versus nation,
Striving to settle,
Differences on the field of battle;
And peace continues to be an illusion,
A utopian dream of a deranged human;

We continue to strive for military supremacy,
Though history has shown us,
That violence is not the remedy;
Isn't it time we learn that war is not a panacea,
A cure all for our inability,
To live in harmony;
And peace continues to be an illusion,
A utopian dream of a deranged human;

Despite man's claim of super-intelligence,
He refuses to listen,
To the dictates of a moral conscience,
The vast majority are blinded,
By the disease of materialism,
Sons and daughters of narcissism;
And peace continues to be an illusion,
A utopian dream of a deranged human;

In man's quest for survival,
Animosity has now become,
A daily ritual,
In today's society,
Is either kill or be killed,
That seems to be the new philosophy;
Yet peace continues to be an illusion,
The utopian dream of a deranged human.

Homeless

Mother and daughter,
Not alone,
Children –
Of society's selfishness and greed,
Whose plight no one truly pays heed;

Children –
Of trembling and doubt,
Whose sustenance, are benevolence and handout;

Mother and daughter,
Not alone,
Children –
Of trauma and sorrow,
No guarantees for tomorrow;

Children –
Of injustice and national short-sightedness,
Hapless off springs of such maladroit-ness;

Mother and daughter,
Not alone,
Children –
Of misery,
Who are innocent, yet guilty;

Children –
Of a perpetual imbalance,
Who from birth had no chance;

Mother and daughter,
No alone,
Children –
Of a now emerging universal family,
Whose numbers are increasing rapidly;

Children –
Fostered, fathered by the new technological order,
Slowly dissipating morals and culture.

Enigma

Where,
Is the joy that life should possess?
Gone,
It seems,
Vanished ....
Into nothingness;

Where,
Are sounds of human frivolity?
Silenced,
It seems,
Quieted ....
Nothing but fear and anxiety;

Where,
Is life's harmony, it rhapsody?
Discord,
Noise ....
No beat or melody;

Where,
Are the people?
I used to know?
Robots,
Victims,
Of the status quo;

Where,
Does it all lead too?
Oblivion,
It seems,
Ignorance ....
Is anyone paying heed?

Reality

Tick tock,
Life dances on with the clock,
Each minute cloaked in uncertainty;

Amidst the grime,
Time moves unobstructed,
Determined;

Memories of yesterday,
They linger and taunt,
Our dreams they haunt;

Opportunities gone,
Naked, wasted,
No time to be debated;

Change,
The inevitable,
The undeniable.

The Reality of Dreams

To dream, to dream,
It's natural,
It's human;
Dreams are the eyes of the future,
The doors that open and unlock the soul's desire,
The pathways that give direction amidst
confusion

To dream,
It's natural,
It's human,
Dreams are the mind's speculative analysis,
Its subconscious awareness,
Of idealistic perspectives;

Dreams, dreams,
The horizons, which give birth to a new day,
They illuminate the way,
Eradicating the obscurities and delusions,
Of blank hope,
And lost opportunity;

To dream, to dream,
It's natural,
It's human,
Dreams the product of an active mind,
Not content with the mundane,
But seeks the highest heights to attain;

Dreams, dreams,
The foundations of idealism,
As the mind tries to structure,
Give meaning to the future,
In expectant fulfillment,
Of needs and aspirations'

To dream,
It's natural,
It's human,
Dreams paint,
Mental pictures,
Of inner desires,
Which hover on the threshold of reality;

Dreams, dreams,
It's healthy,
To give the mind liberty,
Freedom to explore,
And restore,
Meaning and dimension,
To the somewhat nebulousness of life.

This Modern Life, Another Look

In retrospection,
It seems,
Like a perilous journey,
Disaster,
Destruction,
Annihilation ....
Imminent;

The pendulum of time swings,
We act like puppets,
But are we?
Is there no solution?
To this seeming madness,
To the reality of future shock;

We act oblivious,
Frivolous,
Striving to obscure reality,
The implications,
Behind a world of illusions,
No true reality or permanence,
Just decadence ....

We walk as dead men and women,
Haunted,
By phantoms, effigies, and nightmares,
Doomed, damned,
As corpus delicti,
Ready for the pathologist;

Our faces burst with laughter,
But what lies behind the painted smile?
Faces, empty, not a drop of real life,
Preoccupied with the remnants;
The ashes of the beauty,
That once bloomed;

Failure,
Frustration,
Existential madness,
Utter blindness,
Selfish passions,
Crazy reactions,
To fill the void;

We search for freedom,
But where/
Evasive,
Illusive,
An abstract concept,
Invisible,
Unattainable.

Modern Life

So spasmodic, erratic,
And grossly pluralistic,
No heterogeneity,
Or homogeneity,
But disparity,
Mass dissimilation,
Dissension,
Social inconsistency,
Moral intricacy;

Non-conformism,
Tokenism,
Political schism,
Narcissism,
Scientific fanaticism;

Prodigality,
Despite blatant poverty,
Everywhere improbity,
Legal partiality,
Criminosis,
Hedonistic psychosis,
Paranoia;

Schizophrenia,
Pathological personality,
A synthetic society,

Pornographic addiction,
Reprobation;
Extra-terrestrial obsession,
Iconoclasticism,
Religious cynicism,
And skepticism,
Myopia,
Theatrical behavior,
Despite imminent disaster.

The Playground

No more screams, laughter,
Or cries of alarm,
Just a numbing playful silence;

The voices are hushed now,
Gone, blown away,
By a wind of expediency,

A lonely yellow slide calls,
It seems to know my name,
But I do not answer;

The monkey bars,
With swinging arms beckon,
But I am nonchalant, reluctant;

The wooden tree houses invite,
But they too, fail to excite and incite,
My playfulness.

Paradoxes

Why do the good people suffer redress?
While the less favorable,
The wicked, live,
And continue to oppress;

Why do governments spend billions on the military?
So much money! For peace and security,
Creating strife and disparity,
While their poor live in perpetual want;

Why does the rich man's wealth increase?
While the poor,
The less fortunate,
Is on a spiraling decrease;

Why do the children continually suffer?
From hunger and abuse,
When they are the future,
Off springs of a generation, who think violence is the answer;

Why does religion continue to preach and teach?
An ancient proclamation,
Cries in the wilderness,
To an un-persuadable generation;

Why does science, despite its innovation?
Still has no answer, no solution,
To the basic problem of love,
That yet plagues man;

Why, why .... ?
Is there a universal answer?
A consensus of opinion,
Or is the fault in the mirror's reflection?

You and Me

What is important to me,
May not be important to you,
Because I think I am me,
And you think you are you,
We continually see ourselves,
As different,
But are we?

Thoughts, Ideas,
Which keep us separated,
<u>Branches</u>, on a divided tree,
Imaginable ethnic, feminine, masculine,
And cultural leaves,
Blow!
In the fields of discontentment,
Fences, lines of demarcation -
Divide, and cut -
Deep wounds of separation,
Yet I continue to be me,
And you remain you.

Social Commentary

'Where is the love we should possess?
Vanished it seems into nothingness.'

Letter From the Homeless

If you felt my pain,
Or listen as I complain,
Utilizing words and actions to articulate,
My twisted fate;
Instead of judging,
You would be more empathetic to my suffering;

Just yesterday,
I had a place to stay,
Troubles! Far away;
Now, nothing can eliminate,
Or sedate,
Existential insanity,
And the emptiness, deep inside of me;

Now, I a resident of the street,
Tattered shoes, tortured feet;
The waste basket,
My next meal ticket;
Clothes, from the shelter I inherit,
Haphazardly the fit;

In a painted window is a reflection,
An urban apparition,
No semblance,
But a faded resemblance,
A face – familiar,
Now a pitiful picture

Somehow,
I wish you would have a clear conception,
As to the seriousness of my situation,
Is it that I've become so familiar?
Endemic to this culture,
That I am seen as part of the architecture,
Of a decaying structure;
Please adjust your value system,
That's the crux of the problem,
Abandon materialism,
Cultivate altruism,
And there would be less like me,
To intimidate your sanity.

Thinking About the Children

Where, where are the children?
How can they play?
When can they enjoy the bliss of innocence?
If they are not free from the assaults of ignorance,
How can they learn tolerance?

How can they embrace the fullness of living?
When life's examples are animosity and loathing,
If the norm is blatant disrespect and mental thralldom,
How can they learn to value freedom?

How can they respond favorably to a world in need?
When much of their experience
is selfishness and greed,
If this is the attitude, the response to indigence,
How can they learn benevolence?

How can they be responsible men and women?
When morals and ethics are situational,
If violence, war and hatred is the predilection,
How can they learn that love is a better option?

How can they be children?
When they are thrust into adult roles,
If they have been parented by
ignorance, lust and addiction,
How can they learn that truth is the only solution?
The children, tomorrow's people, yesterday's dreams,
How can they aspire to the heights
of human achievement?

When the majority of life's examples
are adversely different,
If this is all life to their empty cups can give,
How can they learn, but what they live?

Have You Seen My Son?

Have you seen my son?
I hear the sirens wail,
Oh! The anguish and pain,
I look for my son, my sibling,
But to no avail;

The staccato sounds of gunshots,
Gasps! The cries of onlookers,
Did my teachings, my warnings,
Fall on deaf ears,
Was he mislead?

Have you seen my son?
I see the law enforcers,
Weapons cocked and ready,
To mete out their brand of justice,
Self-preservation is all that matters;

The blood clotting on the sidewalk,
Is that the ties of our lineage?
The chains! The handcuffs!
Are those the links to the future?

Have you seen my son?
I shout in desperation,
My dreams, my hopes,
The one I nurtured.
But no one listens, their minds in derision.

The ambulance now a distant blur,
A trembling in my heart,
Misgiving, foreboding,
I can't comprehend why?
But! Have you seen my son?

Innocent Ones

Look at them,
Eagerly they rise,
They leave home bent on violence,
With callous indifference,
They are feared, and dreaded,
By mature ones;

They assemble at a common haunt,
Like flies on decaying food,
Ready to solicit the illicit;
They laugh at law and order,
Guilty ones –
Whose strength is in their pockets;

They destroy morals,
Create strife,
They sow and water the seeds of addiction,
Enslaved by a paper God,
Their earnings are blown away,
By a covetous wind;

Their lives are fragments,
Submerged in arrogance and indiscipline,
Misguided, mislead,
Betrayed by – THINGS,
Their lives are 'nothing',
Empty as an overturned cup.

Nightmare!

Stones for my pillow,
Cardboard for a bed,
No permanent place to rest my head;
Who cares about me?
Forsaken by family,
Relentlessly I trod each street,
Tattered shoes, tortured feet,

Winter through fall,
No friend on whom I dare call,
Dusk to dawn, fear and foreboding,
Got to exist by begging,
Jousting the elements of wind and rain,
Hoping in hope to relieve the pain;

Stones for my pillow,
Cast out, disdained by society,
A cruel reality,
Not even laws that deems mercy,
Who could have proclaimed such a decree?
Fate or destiny,
Please somebody, answer ME.

The Wall

Every which way,
A wall,
Tall,
A hindrance,
No cracks,
Or visible signs of weakness,
Not even a blemish;

Just a wall,
Tall,
I miniature, small,
Encircling, engulfing,
A compassionless obstruction,
Fueling my frustration;

A wall,
Tall,
I miniature, small,
On whom could I call?
Such an ominous foreboding structure,
How can I escape?
Hope, my only ladder.

The Writing Is On The Wall

Ashes to ashes, dust to dust,
Time to address that which affect us,
In what do we now place our trust?
Values blown away by a corruptive wind gust,
Lives ruled by greed and lust,
Morals and ideals allowed to rust;

Our sports heroes,
Immersed in their own troubles,
Your idols and role models –
Do they care about your struggles?
Just ready to amass quick dollars,
By endorsing brand name cereals and sneakers;

Tripping off on dope,
Struggling to cope,
Your life on a psychological tightrope,
Clutching at straws, a life built on empty hope,
At illusions you grope,
But they too disappear like a puff of smoke;

No respect,
Just disrespect,
Your actions towards the sisters you should inspect,
Misuse, abuse of the opposite sex,
No appreciation – male domination
of the females you select,
Their determination and contribution you reject;

Immersed in self pity,
Blinded, you thrive on enmity,
Believing yourself to be a victim of society,
Tunnel vision, mental frailty,
Ignorant, oblivious – no self-respect or dignity,
Ethnic calamity;

Within you, the fires of hate burn,
Like hungry children, mothers and daughters yearn,
That from a legacy of violence you'll turn,
And perhaps the truth you'll discern,
From the examples of others you may learn,
You need to educate your mind to earn;

Smiling faces, masking plots,
Hanging out in familiar spots,
Flashing in modern chariots,
Ready to take from the have- nots,
Jealousy, lies and deceit to feed the slots,
Your lives tied up in knots.

Just One Wish

Sometimes I wish,
I could crawl into a shell,
When life is not swell,
A place faraway,
Just to hide away;

My own secret place,
A place to rendezvous,
When I am sad and blue,
Just somewhere 'to be',
Alone with unhappy me.

I Hear A Cry!

I hear a cry,
Out there!
Where, hoping is hopeless

Painful,
Desperate,
Passionate,

I hear a cry,
Out there!
Where, greed leaves many powerless,

Mournful,
Piercing,
Haunting,

I hear a cry,
Out there!
Where, poverty's face is ageless,

Forceful,
Echoing,
Demanding,

I hear a cry,
Out there!
Where, too many are homeless,
I hear a cry.

Life on the Edge

In an overpopulated world,
It's easy to be lonely,

Callous, unfriendly and often devious,
It's easy to be lonely,

Too many exist on charitableness,
It's easy to be lonely,

Prejudice, greed and avarice,
It's easy to be lonely,

Selfishness, conditional happiness,
It's easy to be lonely,

Suicide, abnormal increase in homicide,
It's easy to be lonely,

Prodigality, despite worldwide poverty,
It's easy to be lonely,

Substance abuse and misuse,
It's easy to be lonely.

Shattered Dreams

Woman!
I can hear
Your silent screams,
Visions of your shattered dreams,
Reverberates in my heart,
As that which was so priceless,
Now mingles with the dust;

Woman!
Searching,
Hoping to recover,
From the disaster,
Some relic or treasure,
To perhaps measure,
That which bloomed before;

Woman!
So many tedious years,
Now tears,
Disclose your inner fears,
All gone –
Nature's swift verdict,
Executed by a merciless wind;

Woman!
What do you hope to salvage?
From such wanton wreckage,
Of dreams and hopes,
Now dead;
Eulogized in silt and grime,
What was your crime?

Woman!
Is there someone looking?
Who perhaps can shed some light?
Answers to your plight;
One who will offer words,
Not of lament,
But enough, to soothe the wounds
of your predicament.

Mislead

Little boy,
Innocent,
Young man, unspoiled,
I used to know;
Now!
Child of a sub-culture;

No more golden smiles,
Tears,
For seven decreed years,
But who really cares?
Maturity will come quickly;

In tried to warn,
Amidst the shadows,
Empty words –
Like drops of water,
In a desert,

Of loneliness,
Of false identities,
Of greed,
Of misguidance,
Of low self-esteem;

No direction,
False motivation,
No roots to hold on to,
Another statistic of the system,
How many more, before we address the problem?

After the Smoke Clears

(This poem was written after the Rodney King verdict and
subsequent Los Angeles Riots in 1991.)

After the smoke clears,
Is there going to be a new agenda?
Will the waters have truly quenched the FIRES?
Oh! How they burned,
The flames some say long overdue;

After the smoke clears,
Will the message be finally heard?
After centuries of political rhetoric,
What wounds would've been bandaged?
Will the flames have burned away division and strife?
Exposing our basic humanity, uplifting human dignity;

After the smoke clears,
Will we find the ashes of prejudice and injustice?
Will we uncover the scorched
remains of hatred and racism?
The tree of bigotry, will it be charred to its roots?
In this wilderness –
Will the embers provide fertility for barren hope?

After the smoke clears,
Can we emphatically say?
To hate and injustice,
Inequality and prejudice,
Deceit and malice,
Ashes to ashes,
Dust to dust.

Enigma of A Lady

Stone cold lady,
In placid sobriety,
Beckoning,
Jousting the elements,
That would obliterate,
And efface the records;

Blizzards,
Turbulent winds of change,
Shaking,
Threatening to topple over,
To shatter,
Immigrant dreams;

Stone cold lady,
Castigated by waves of delusion,
Showers of discontent,
Confusion,
Storms of racism,
Subtle unrest,
Put the LADY to a test;

Frost bitten,
Chilling times of moral decadence,
Mists, and fog,
Obscure,
As bigotry, and prejudice masquerade,
Beclouding the light;

Stone cold lady,
Tainted by lost hope,
Spiraling winds of distrust,
Myriads of dreams that died,
With the ebb and flow of the tide,
Crushed on the rocks of greed;

Stone cold lady,
Eroded, enshrouded,
Cracked,
Quaking from distrust,
Yet striving to equate,
And restore the DREAM.

People

People,
Ascending
Descending,
Others on level ground,
People all around;

Modern, automated people,
Impatient, resilient,
Polluted people;

People,
Forgotten, forsaken,
Careless, helpless,
Hungry, dirty,
People, refused, confused;

Devious, nervous,
Frenzied, hurried,
Guarded, assimilated,
Defensive people;

People,
Worried, harried,
Contemplative, addictive,
Neurotic, organic,
Ordinary, everyday people.

Dear Brother and Sister

Where is the love you pretend to possess?
When you say, hey! Brother or sister,
But mug and rip me off,
Sell my stuff for a quick dollar,
To satisfy your twisted desire;

How about you sister?
You sell your body for want of money,
Where is that African dignity?
You talk about women's liberation,
But is your mind really free?

Where is your pride, your self-dignity?
You complain about oppression and racial inequality,
But you are like a vulture,
Selling illicit drugs and robbing your poor,
You'll do anything for money,
Just the way the system wants you to be;

Disco, party,
Night life, that's your thing,
To be in the swing!
Can't see the broken homes,
The financial waste,
Frustration, loneliness,
Driving your further into social oblivion,
No self motivation;

Where is your sense of value?
You live in subsidized apartments,

Your eyes larger than your pockets,
Always in debt,
Mimicking the rich and famous,
Few are serious about self-sacrifice,
Mixed signals I am getting,
Who are you really hurting?

What could you contribute towards Black society?
When your life is beset with so much malady,
You spend most of your life in a 'ghetto',
Holding up street corners,
Trying to get over, or under,
Few of you ever finish school,
And you think that's cool!

Somebody Cares

Somebody cares about you,
Despite feelings of loneliness,
Life's apparent coldness,
Out there!
In the vast somewhere,
Someone wants to share;

Somebody cares about you,
Though broken promises, failures, lost opportunity,

Make you suspicious and angry,
There is one,
Who –
Will yet stand by you;

Somebody cares about you,
Through daily uncertainty,
Recurring guilt and anxiety,
LOOK! And you'll see,
A helping hand reaching out,
For you to hold, and cast away all doubt;

Somebody cares about you,
Even in the valley of depression,
Frustration, no self-motivation,
Don't turn off the light,
But fight!
Fight you must,
Humans are not all devious,
There is someone you can learn to trust;

Somebody cares about you,
You may not fully comprehend why,
But even when you cry,
Because of another trial,
You are special,
Incomparable, without pair,
Everyday of the year,
January through December,
Remember,
Somebody cares about you.

City of the Dead

Amidst the ruins,
I search,
For some semblance, a missing link,
A tangible reminder,
But all I uncover are broken, twisted artifacts,
Nostalgic memoirs;

Grief cries out like a banshee,
From a forest of decayed walls and debris,
Residual droppings of materialism,
Enshrouded in clinging vines,
Yesterday a sad anomaly,

The earth toasted into a dusty almond,
Bleached white stones,
Carpet a once friendly landscape,
Trees – skeletal replicas,
Poignant reminders,
As decadence reigns;

No more morals or mores,
Laws or restrictions,
No hopes, or dreams,
No pain, or sorrow,
Just a numbing, barren emptiness.

Existential Poems

'I am not what you believe me to be'

To Be Me

To be me,
I am determined to be,
In the city,
Wherever I may be,
I will be me.

Even in the city,
In the midst of poverty,
Crime, high technology,
Antipathy,
I will be me.

I will not lose me,
In the city,
Haven of artificiality,
The greedy,
Moral impartiality,
Endemic to the city,
Beckoning, trying to seduce me.

The city,
Characteristic of monotony,
Unending industry,
Plural complexity,
Shaping, molding me,
With its malignancy,
And lack of continuity.

The city,
Seeped in impersonality,

*Lost in the majority,
Loosing my sanctity,
But I will be me,
Even in the city.*

I Am Not Me

I am not what you believe me to be,
What you see,
Is but a physical body,
That which gives me notoriety,
In the face of society;

Do not define me by this physical identity,
Because I am not what you think you see,
Accomplishments, achievements, do not define me,
Neither do academic or social status capture,
The essence of my true identity,
My higher self that is beyond the realm of visibility;

I am not my thoughts which flow incessantly,
Across the sky of my mind as examine closely,
Anger, greed, jealousy, spite, cruelty, lust, fear and anxiety,
Mind and body do live eternally,
This could never be my true identity;

I am not my race, religion or country,
Trinidadian, naturalized American,
May be my ascribed nationality,
But yet these terms fail to capture me,
An eternal spirit, formless without a single boundary,
Ethnic or cultural identity;

Teacher, preacher, computer operator, psychologist,
Names, labels, occupational titles,
Is that really me?

I have to be more, than the jobs I do,
Neither am I the doer,
Just the silent, impartial observer.

Searching

Who am I?
Where the cold winds blow,
Not like the winds I used to know,
Yet I yearn to find me,
My self-identity;

Who am I?
Dream or reality,
In midst of social inequality,
Decadence, and moral decay,
Searching for a way –
Amidst paranoia and schizophrenia;

Who am I?
In the midst of this nightmarish frenzy of life,
Existential strife,
Universal madness,
Conditional happiness,
Sojourner or stranger,
Or created creature?

Who am I?
Man,
Beast, or biological entity,
In an uncharted madness,
Where many are clueless,
To the obvious;

Who am I?
Puppet, robot or player,

Programmed by tradition and culture,
Yet determined to find me,
My potentiality,
No matter what besets me;

Who am I?
My ancestral ties are long,
Across the distant seas,
Drums beat a familiar song,
Calling!
Messages to my soul,
Is this who I am?
Or is it the memory,
Of who I used to be?

Leave Me In The Dark

Leave me in the dark,
Lest the light,
Thrust my sanity into fright,
As it discloses the unevenness
Of life, void of true happiness,
Humans ignoring the obvious,
While wars' haunting spectra,
Invades every culture;

Leave me in the dark,
Lest I see,
The creeping hand of global poverty,
With elongated fingers,
Traversing ancient barriers,
As populations increase rapidly,
And food becomes a scarce commodity;

Leave me in the dark.
Lest the light illuminate,
The terrorism, the hate,
Which science cannot obliterate,
Or with theories sedate,
But stand like modern enigmas,
Eroding the very structure –
While humans on the political table,
Shuffled, swapped, expendable;

Leave me in the dark,
Lest I see,
The painted faces,

Insidious smiles, seeking social graces;
City streets void of passion,
Beings in commotion,
Methodical confusion,
Images in a nightmarish apparition;

Leave me in the dark,
Lest the bulb enshroud,
The descending cloud,
The marks of social injustice,
Centuries of systematic depravation,
Endemic to every generation;

Leave me in the dark,
For light serves little purpose,
As we continually fail to see US,
Leave me in the dark,
Where it is fortuitous,
To grope in uncertainty,
Than live in a world, where, few can really see.

Beggar-man

Beggar-man,
That you should come,
Into my life,
Standing ....
In my way,
Clothes dirty and raggedy,

Disclosing, unearthing,
The dark side,
Feelings stir,
Emotion, compassion,
That which I thought was dead,
Eulogized by hate and distrust,
Mingling with the corruptive dust,
Now resurrected;

How dare you?
Transgress my freedom,
Imploring,
Beseeching benevolence,
Hoping,
That perchance ....
Appealing to my soul,
My communal spirit;

Go away!
Don't impinge
Or open scars,
Wounding –
Go away!
I hate you.

Poetic Dilemma

Timelessly I search,
For themes of joy, and laughter;
But how could I write,
Or dare to invite?
The reader to such,
When life's discord is so much;

How could I write?
Or describe the beauty of a flower,
While my brothers and sisters suffer,
Denied their rights,
Their individuality,
An opportunity to BE;

How could I put pen to paper?
Invoke the beauty of a nature,
While there are those who hunger,
And die daily,
A universal malady,
Continually haunting me;

How could I describe?
The radiance of the sunlight,
While there are those who fight,
For what is theirs' by ancestral right,
Exploited, controlled by might,
While the majority ....
Unconcerned by such blatant depravity;

How could I write?
Though I try to concentrate,
My pen cannot beauty captivate,
On joy and happiness I cannot focus,
When so much is out of locus,
Modern life hovering on the extremity,
Of pluralistic insanity;

How could I write?
Verses in iambic meter,
Expressing in vivid imagery,
Utilizing metaphor and simile,
To describe a moonlit sky,
When daily I hear the poor cry,
Tears, staining,
Marring –
Indelible marks of injustice,
Social and racial prejudice;

No, no I cannot write,
But with words I'll fight,
Through moral and subtle persuasion,
I'll comment,
And perhaps the world will lament,
For the innumerable who muddle in sorrow,
Holding on to fragile dreams,
Clinging on, to a hapless tomorrow.

Let the Music Play

Let the music play!
Let it soothe,
The disharmony,
The morbid malady
Of another tomorrow,
Shipwrecked on the shores of sorrow;

Let the music play,
LOUD!
Let the vibes enshroud,
The clamor of discontent,
As the oppressors continue to torment,
Riding on the backs of the poor,
Human dignity and benevolence they ignore;

Let the music play!
Let the scintillating vibration,
The pulsation,
Quell the sounds of human savagery,
Creature rivalry,
In the midst of national and political irony;

Let the music play!
Let the melody,
Of each major and minor key,
Transport me –
FAR! From this insanity,
To a future reality,
Where there is homo-sapiens harmony.

The Traveler

In this journey of life,
I am a solitary traveler,
Across the steep hills and valleys of disappointments,
I have endured;

But traveling on,
To the exits of desire and self-passion,
Across the rugged footpaths of hope,
Lost opportunity,
Yet I have endured;

Traveling on,
No entry to right the wrongs,
One way!
Towards the intersections of decision and commitment,
Yet I have endured;

Still traveling,
Through the speed limits,
Of moral and social expectations,
Tried to rationalize and negotiate the detours,
Of broken dreams, my human frailties,
Yet I have endured;

Traveling on to the stop sign of circumstances,
No time to retrospect or reconstruct,
The dead ends of love,
Destiny beckons,
The journey must continue,
Therefore I endure,

Instinctively I travel,
Along this twisted highway,
Littered with broken dreams,
Punctuated with curves of suspense,
But nothing will deter,
Though time, my aged friend slowly becomes my foe.

Heart Songs

*Lord where would I be?
Imprisoned in mortality,
My life, certain uncertainty,
Alienated, in disharmony;*

*Though guilty,
Where would I be?
But for love unconditional,
I now hope in things eternal;*

*Oh! Lord where would I be?
If you hadn't paid the penalty,
Obscured by sin's indelible stain,
Yet grace did not disdain,*

*Frail, finite me,
Lord where would I be?
Although far, I had wondered,
Yet the blood covered;*

*Lord where would I be?
If you didn't delight in mercy,
When right, I was so wrong,
But Jesus you came along;*

*If you didn't snatch me,
Just where would I be
From the depths of sin,,
Destined to perish therein;*

*Now with you I am more assured about tomorrow,
Not burdened with bitterness and sorrow,
If your love didn't flow,
Where I would be
Lord, I don't know?*

I'd Rather Be Blind

I'd rather be blind,
Than gaze upon
The pictures life paints around me.
The world's people going around in circles,
Like a play land Ferris Wheel,
BLINDED! By jealousy and suspicion –
Twentieth century tunnel vision;

I'd rather be blind,
As there are too many with sight,
Who can't truly see;
Men and women
Wearing the spectacles of lust and greed,
BLINDED! By selfish conjunctiva
Modern myopia;

I'd rather be blind, than view lifestyles of the rich and famous,
Such wantonness, an obscenity –
On starvation they never focus,
They are BLINDED!
By materialism, politics and academia,
Victims of economic esotropia;

I'd rather be blind,
And grope in the dark,
Suffer the indignity of being sightless,
Than be like those who look askance,
As they continually disdain,
And practice ethnocentrism,

BLINDED! By centuries of dichromaticism;
I'd rather be blind,
Than view life's adversity,
Nations in futile rivalry,
Covetous, boastful and proud,
Leaders – seeing but sightless,
BLINDED! By distorted images in a political mirror,
And corruptive astigmia;

I'd rather be blind,
Unless people everywhere,
All the world's children,
Put on the contact lens of peace and love,
Look through the eyes of patience and temperance,
And create a world where all men can TRULY SEE,
I'd rather be blind.

The Watcher

I've looked at life and what do I see,
A crazy reckless world,
Hurtling to its rendezvous with destiny;

I've looked across the endless ocean of time and space,
Searching, seeking beauty in this human race,
But all I see –
Is the looming head of hate and poverty;

I've looked at man's version of love,
Incomparable with that from above,
Mere human and physical fantasy,
Real and true
But passes like the morning dew;

I've looked for a real friend,
One who will stand by you,
Even to the end;
But what do I see,
Friends are often conditional,
Not to be depended on in a time of trial;

I've looked at man,
The highest they say of all creation,
But what do I see,
Corruption and destruction,
A multitude of modern technological invention,
But still no solution,
To the real problem
ALIENATION.

My Soul Looks Back And Wonder

My soul looks back and wonder,
How I got over?
Across the perilous seas of life,
Inner strife,
I look back and wonder,
How I got over?

When my life was seeped in sin,
Doubts and fears surged within,
My soul can't help but wonder,
How I got over?

Though I tried repeatedly,
To right the wrongs,
To undo which was done with sincerity,
All my efforts did but fail,
A waste, all to no avail,
Yet I got over,
Human feat or God's grace? I wonder,
How did I make it over?

Self here, self there,
Self everywhere,
How did I make it over?
My soul looks back and wonder,
How did I really get over?

When I wanted to do right,
Evil was ever present,
No strength to fight,

Oblivious to the real predicament,
But somehow I got over,
Somehow I made it through,
By God's mercy I am a winner,
My soul looks back .....
Can't help but wonder?

Miscellaneous Poems

'Whatever, promotes the dignity of all men,
Ensures justice and equality ....
Think on these things.'

There is a Mouse in My Room

There is a mouse in my room,
Causing me nothing but gloom,
Somehow it climbs up on my table,
Such a bold little fellow,
I never knew he was able.

He chewed open my favorite pack of crackers,
I did not invite him,
But I don't think that really matters;

He made such a great bit mess,
Strewing crumbs,
All over my desk,
What a rude,
Uninvited guest!

If I should catch him there,
I would give him a real big scare,
BOO!
He won't come back for more,
I am sure.

Shoes

Shoes,
For eager feet,
Where are you going,
To take me today?
Who will we meet?

Brown shoes,
We are old friends,
Comfortable,
Wherever I go,
Even in snow –
Summer's heat,
Gentle on my feet.

Shoes,
Brown and polished,
Smooth and laced,
Like the day you were born,
Reliable,
And so comfortable;
These shoes I love,
I think you fell from above,
Lets take a walk.

Rain

Let the rain fall,
Let the cascading showers,
Wash away,
The grime,
The slime;

Let the rain fall,
Let the crystal drops,
Paint,
Wet pictures,
Glittering caricatures,
On my window;

Let the rain fall,
Let its cool waters,
Quench,
The desires,
The yearnings,
Of a thirsty world.

Haiku

Big bulb
Burning bright
Shine for me
Your blinding light.

My Son's Birth

   Amidst
       The
           Throngs
               Of pain,
                  And
                     The
                        Loud
                           Verbal
                              Persuasions

A grayish
     Form
         Thrust
            Its
               Slimy
                  Body
                     Into
                        A
                           Waiting
                              World .

Clouds

Distant puffs
Dream lazily,
In a bed of blue,
Like crazy marshmallow creatures,
Waiting! To pounce on you;

Curious shapes,
Float menacingly,
Camouflaged in coats of white,
No haste, to their
Apparent flight

Poetry

A
  Poem
    Is
      Like
        A
          Drop
            Of
              Water
In
  A
    Desert
      Of
        Emotion,
          Frustration,
            And
              Loneliness.

Snow

Cold curious
White shapes,
Descending
To
The bare
Waiting
Ground.

The Rain

The rain feels,
Like nature's
Cool gift,
Falling
                        From
                          A
                            Happy
                              Sky.

The Musical Rain

The rain,
Drums its sweet melody,
On my window pane,
Calling me to come outside,
But I run and hide.

Like a drummer
It beats a persistent melody,
Window rhapsody,
My special lullaby,
As I struggle not to shut my eye.

Waiting for Spring

I wait and watch for spring,
And the carpets of flowers
It would bring;

But winter stands, like a mean cold giant,
Defiant,
Blocking the way;

I wait and watch for spring,
No more snow,
Like huge mountains of forgotten dough;

But soon the birds will sing,
Like little musicians,
Their proclamations of spring;

I wait and watch for spring,
When my heart will dance and sing,
In April's sun, as winter is forced,
Finally to run.

Winter and Me

I love the crunchy piles of fresh white snow,
Not the cold unfriendly winds,
That howl as they blow.

I love building a big bellied snowman,
With a carrot for a nose,
All he wears is hat and scarf for clothes;

I don't like to see unhappy trees,
Seems like someone has stolen their leaves,
But I love to sip on sweet hot chocolate,
And drink soup with lentil peas.

I don't like when my nose freeze,
And the cold makes me sneeze,
And my face feels like Swiss cheese.

Pages

Inviting,
Enticing,
Waiting,
For words;

But the white void,
Seems impenetrable,
As thoughts skip,
Restless,
Like a naughty child in a toy store,
Disobedient,
Rebellious,
From azaleas to Australia,
To umbrellas, to yaks,
And zebras;

But I wait,
And watch them,
Eager for some syllabic representation,
Of my mind's contemplation.

The Wind and Me

Today was not as cold as yesterday,
Yesterday the wind was angry,
Scolding the trees and their branches,
And the big old garbage cans,
Plastic bottles, paper bags,
And old rags were all beaten up,
But the wind would not stop.

Cold and unfriendly,
An invisible monster without pity,'
Come think, it was mad at everybody,
A dog, an old lady,
All felt its fury,
Including me;
It tried to steal my coat,
Wrapped my scarf around my throat;

Oh! He was mad,
I ran inside when he tried
To steal my hat,
No! wind you can't have that.

Nostalgia

Just yesterday you were here,
I didn't know the meaning of fear,
Now despair;
Nothing but the icy hand of loneliness,
A numbing barren emptiness,
Unfriendly,
Bottomless,
Beckoning,
To my sanity calling,
Trying to entice me,
Across, the great darkness

Dreams

Dreams are like the steering wheel of a car,
Without them, you won't get far,
Strive with all your might,
Your life, just won't be right;

Dreams, the fuel in life's tank,
They are like money in the bank,
They give you the power to achieve,
If you'll only, in yourself, believe.

Dreams, the wheels around which our lives rotate,
The future they help you navigate,
Giving us the momentum to BE,
As we ride high, on the clouds of expectancy.

Journey

Out of the teaming jungles,
The looming tropical forests,
Of a continent "dark",
They came,
To live, multiply,
Labor and forget;

Not by choice,
But by barter,
Cultural betrayal,
And capture,
As merchandise, stocked,
Stacked, on a wind vessel;

Across turbulent seas,
Uncertain, uneasy,
Freedom a mindless thing,
Days of repugnant odors,
Spirits bruised, battered,
Fearfully they waited,
As eyes stared helpless, hopeless
Into a darkness,
That matched their skin tone;

To a new world,
Pompous, cold and heartless,
As chattel property,
Where the sugar-cane, tobacco,
Cacao and cotton grew,
To work and work,

Toil and toil,
Till the sun went to sleep,
Longing, yearning,
For a taste of the past.

When I was Little

When I was little I was afraid of the sea,
Now! No one can swim as fast me.

When I was little I was afraid of lighting and thunder,
Now! They are not even a bother.

When I was little everywhere I went the moon would follow,
Now! I know he wasn't really such a persistent fellow.

When I was little I thought there were monsters and goblins,
Now! I know that there are no such frightful things.

When I was little my mom took care of me,
Now! She's gone her face I long to see.

When I was little I waited up all night for the tooth fairy,
Now! I know that she is just a fantasy.

When I was little I just couldn't get my shoes on right,
Now! We never have to fight.

When I was little I longed to be older, to grow up,
Now! It seems as though this process will never stop.

Spring

<u>S</u>weet, sassy and sensational,
<u>P</u>romising, particular and positive,
<u>R</u>adiant, resplendent and rhythmic,
<u>I</u>dyllic, irresistible and invigorating,
<u>G</u>reen, glamorous, gorgeous and giving.

Dem Dun Forget

How soon dem people forget Martin,
And all de sixties protestin and marchin
Ah tell yuh, dem forget yes,
Dem dun forget.

Dem forget all dem songs of freedom,
How dey use to ride in de back ah de bus,
How dey was lynched and murdered,
Beat up, wet down wih water hose,
How de couldn't cross de line,
How de was pack up,
And put in de paddy wagon;

Now! Dem robbin and rapin,
Dey own black skin,
Sellin and usin de wite powda,
No kinda unity,
Ah wonda if dey really free?

Some playing politiks too,
Only seekin dey own interests,
But dem doh know,
Dem dun forget Martin.

What Do You Want To Be?

What do you want to 'Be'?
Such a great big world,
Out there,
Waiting! For you to see;

There are those who say, you could 'Be',
Whatever your heart dreams of,
Set goals,
And they would soon blossom into reality;

What do you want to 'Be'?
The door of opportunity awaits,
Search, search,
Till you find the key;

Education will help you to 'Be',
Don't quit, or give up,
Never, never stop,
Until you are soaring from the top.

Summer's Heat

Down by the friendly sea,
Is the place to be,
When summer's unfriendly sun,
Forces you from your home to run

One Wish

I wish I had the power,
In every heart to plant the seed of love,
So that,
It may bloom and grow like a beautiful flower.

I will let love wash away,
Centuries of hate, hurt and pain,
In each and every country,
Only love will be king, it would reign;

Could you imagine?
A world devoid of suffering,
Where love like a longed for blanket covers All,
The rich, the mighty, the poor and the small;

No more will the cries of mothers and children,
Pierce the air, like a wailing siren,
Every which way you go,
Love, like the surging waters of river, will flow and flow.

The Education Plan

I am not here to be your enemy,
Or to win a contest in popularity;

I am here to teach, to guide you, my time to invest,
And motivate you to be your best;

Cursing, and unruly behavior I will not accept,
As these are not the attributes of respect;

I am here to enhance the quality of your life,
To help you conquer despair and inner strife;

I cannot, will not accept impudence,
Or those who surrender to indolence;

I am here to free your mind from ages of bondage,
And help you walk along the path of knowledge;

I cannot condone violence and aggression,
They are not part of the education plan;

I am here to help you learn to forgive, the art of toleration,
And create a world void of hatred and aggression.

Wishing for you

Your tantalizing smile,
Wrapped in so much guile,
Oh! And when you step in style,
Resistance is so futile

I savor the moments when we are near,
My heart like a caged bird,
Wrestles with feelings so deep and sincere,
Yet disclosure of this secret is my greatest fear,

About the Author

Martin Richards was born in the twin island Republic of Trinidad and Tobago. He immigrated to the United States in 1978. Martin started teaching at the age of eighteen and continues to be a teacher in Brooklyn, New York. He also started writing poetry about this time on various subjects. Although he has the skill to write about any subject, much of his poetry is about his private philosophical reflections and concerns of life. He has read some of his poetry to public audiences on various occasions. Martin has been somewhat reluctant to publish what he viewed as the private concerns of his heart. This decision finally came after the numerous prompting of friends and colleagues who after hearing or reading his poetry felt he had a voice which was worthy to be heard.

Printed in the United States
44908LVS00005B